WITHDRAWN

PHOENIX-ANNAPOLIS
MEDIA CENTER

A Note to Parents

Eyewitness Readers is a compelling new program for beginning readers, designed in conjunction with leading literacy experts, including Dr. Linda Gambrell, President of the National Reading Conference and past board member of the International Reading Association.

Eyewitness has become the most trusted name in illustrated books, and this new series combines the highly visual *Eyewitness* approach with engaging, easy-to-read stories. Each *Eyewitness Reader* is guaranteed to capture a child's interest while developing his or her reading skills, general knowledge, and love of reading.

The four levels of *Eyewitness Readers* are aimed at different reading abilities, enabling you to choose the books that are exactly right for your children:

Level One – Beginning to read
Level Two – Beginning to read alone
Level Three – Reading alone
Level Four – Proficient readers

The "normal" age at which a child begins to read can be anywhere from three to eight years old, so these levels are intended only as a general guideline.

No matter which level you select, you can be sure that you are helping your child learn to read, then read to learn!

A DK PUBLISHING BOOK
www.dk.com

Project Editor Lara Tankel Holtz
Art Editor Susan Calver
Senior Editor Linda Esposito
Deputy Managing Art Editor Jane H
US Editor Regina Kahney
Production Kate Oliver
Picture Research Jo Carlill
Photographer Lynton Gardiner

Reading Consultant
Linda B. Gambrell, Ph.D.

First American Edition, 1998
2 4 6 8 10 9 7 5 3
Published in the United States by
DK Publishing, Inc.
95 Madison Avenue, New York, New York 10016

Copyright © 1998 Dorling Kindersley Limited, London

All rights reserved under International and Pan-American
Copyright Conventions. No part of this publication
may be reproduced, stored in a retrieval system,
or transmitted in any form or by any means, electronic,
mechanical, photocopying, recording, or otherwise, without
the prior written permission of the copyright owner.

Eyewitness Readers™ is a trademark of
Dorling Kindersley Limited, London.

Published in Great Britain by Dorling Kindersley Limited.

Library of Congress Cataloging-in-Publication Data
Royston, Angela.
    Fire fighters -- 1st American ed.
        p.   cm. -- (Eyewitness readers. Level 2)
    Summary: Describes a day in the life of a group of fire fighters.
    ISBN 0-7894-2960-8
    1. Fire extinction--Juvenile literature. 2. Fire fighters-
-Juvenile literature. [1. Fire extinction. 2. Fire fighters.]
– DK Publishing, Inc. II. Series.
    TH9148.F466   1998
    628.9'25--DC21
                                                                97

Color reproduction by Colorscan, Singapore
Printed and bound in Belgium by Proost.

Special thanks to:
All the fire fighters at Harrison Street Fire Station, New Rochelle
especially Danny Heinz, Anthony Costa, and Thomas Connell;
John Santore of Hook & Ladder 5, and the fire fighters of Engine 24
Hook & Ladder 5, New York City. Thanks also to Liz Radin.
The publisher would like to thank the following for their kind
permission to reproduce their photographs:
t=top, b=below, l=left, r=right, c=center.
Colorific: Ian Bradshaw 23c; **Jim Pickerell** 12c; **Rex:** Cole 14tr;
Greg Williams 25c; **Tony Stone Images:** James McLoughlin 18c.
Colorific: P.F. Bently / Black Star front cover.

EYEWITNESS READERS

Fire Fighter!

Written by Angela Royston

DK PUBLISHING, INC.

It is busy at the fire station
even when there is no fire.
Liz is checking the hoses.
She wants to make sure
they screw tightly to the truck.

Dan is polishing
the fire truck
wheels.

nthony is upstairs
the kitchen,
oking for
snack.
e is always
ungry!
uddenly
loud noise
akes him jump.

Ring!
Ring!
Ring!

It is the fire alarm.
Anthony slides
down the pole.
THUD!
He lands hard.
But the thick
rubber pad
on the ground
cushions his feet.

Ready for action
Pants are kept rolled down over boots to save time. That way the fire fighters can be dressed and in the fire truck in 30 seconds.

z jumps into her boots

nd pulls up her fireproof pants.

ne checks

ne computer.

shows the fire

at 7 Oak Lane.

the truck

iz grabs the

alkie-talkie.

Chief Miller!

We're on

ur way!"

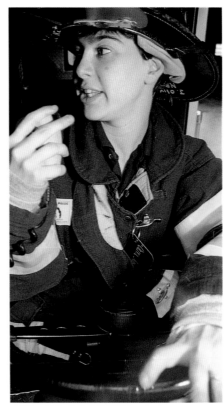

"Right!" says the
fire chief.
He has gone ahead
in a special fast car.
"I'll meet you there."

z starts the engine

the fire fighters jump in.

he flips on the sirens and lights

nd drives out of the fire house.

he truck speeds toward the fire.

Cars and buses stop and wait
when they hear the sirens coming.

The fire chief calls Liz.
"I'm at the fire scene.
It's an old house
that's been empty for years.
But someone saw a young boy
playing on the porch this morning.
He might be inside the house.
Tell Dan and Anthony to
get their air tanks ready."

"Okay, Chief," says Liz.
"I can see the smoke from here.
We'll be there in two minutes."

Liz turns the corner into Oak Lane.
Flames cover the top of the house.

he fire is spreading quickly.
here's no time to lose!

Hoses
Water comes out
of a fire hose
hard enough to
knock a person down.

Liz hooks a hose from the truck
to the nearest fire hydrant.
A pump on the truck pulls water
from the hydrant to another hose.
Liz and another fire fighter
point the hose at the flames.
"Ready!" calls Liz.

WHOOSH! They hold on
tight as water shoots out.

Breathing equipment
Fire gives off deadly smoke.
Fire fighters wear air tanks
and breathing masks inside
a burning building.

Anthony and Dan are ready
to search the house.

They have put on their

air tanks and face masks.

Each tank holds 40 minutes of air.

That's not much time!

"The boy's name is Luke,"
the chief tells them.

"Right," says Anthony.

He grabs a hose.

"Let's put the wet stuff
on the red stuff!" says Dan.

an and Anthony run
the back of the house.
he fire is not as bad here.
an feels the back door.
it is hot, flames could leap out.
t's cold," says Dan.
hey step inside.

hick black smoke is everywhere.
nthony shines his flashlight around.
uke! Luke!" he calls.
o one answers.
can hear fire upstairs," says Dan.
he fire has damaged the staircase.
could fall down at any time.
hey climb up the steps very slowly.

20

Outside, the
outriggers are
set down on
the ground.

Outriggers are like legs.
They keep the truck steady

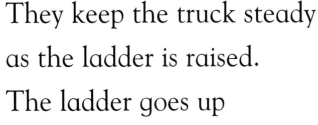

as the ladder is raised.
The ladder goes up
like a telescope
to the top of the house.

A hose runs up the side.
The fire fighter on the ladder
shoots water down on the fire.
The flames crackle and hiss.
They get smaller, then suddenly
jump even higher.

Inside the house, the fire rages.

It is hot enough to melt glass.

Anthony sprays water on the flame

Fire has made the house weak.

"It could come down any second,"

says Dan. "We must find Luke."

BOOM!

A beam crashes down near them.

But their helmets protect their hea

CRASH!

"Quick!" says Anthony.

"We're running out of time."

Hard hats
Fire fighters' helmets
are made of hard plastic.
A wide brim helps to keep
sparks off their necks.

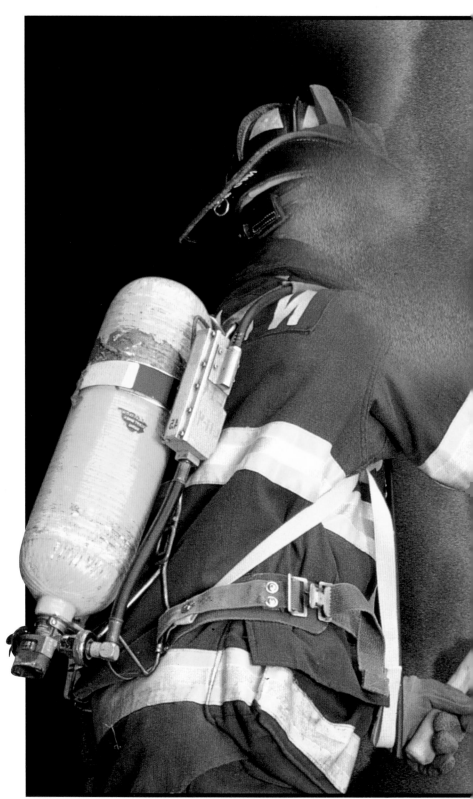

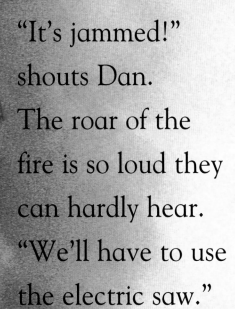

They come to another door.
But it will not open.
Dan swings his axe at the door.
Once. Twice. Three times.
"It's jammed!"
shouts Dan.
The roar of the
fire is so loud they
can hardly hear.
"We'll have to use
the electric saw."

Fire fighters' axe
Axes have been
used by fire fighters
since the earliest days
of fire fighting.

Sharp cutter
The electric saw
runs on batteries.
It can cut right through
the roof of a car
like a can opener.

Anthony switches on the saw.

WHRRR!

He cuts a hole in the door

big enough to climb through.

"Luke!" calls Dan. "Luke?"

But the room is empty.

Suddenly the
chief calls.
"Get out now!
The roof is
coming down!"

Dan and Anthony race downstairs
They get out just as the roof falls i
"We didn't find Luke!" yells Dan.
"He's okay," says the chief.
"We just found him up the block."
"Whew!" says Dan. "Good news!"

ours later
e flames
e out.
nthony sprays
ater on the
rts still
owing red.
e is tired
d dirty –
d very hungry!

Liz winds
the hoses back
on to the truck.
Finally she rests.
She is tired too.

Back at the station
Anthony sits down to eat.
"At last!" he says.

Suddenly a loud noise
makes him jump.
"Dinner will
have to wait!"
laughs Dan.

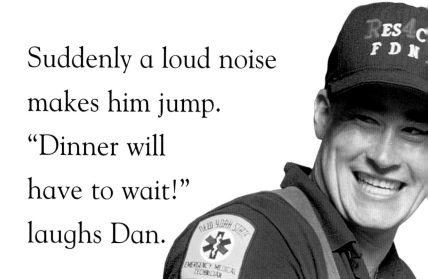

Ring!
Ring!
Ring!

31

PRACTICE E.D.I.T.H. – Exit Drills in the Home

Do you know what to do
if a fire starts in your home?
Don't wait until it happens:

- Sit down with your
  family now.
- Talk about how you
  would get out of
  the house.
- Plan at least two ways
  out of every room.
- Decide where you
  will all meet once
  you get outside.

**A fire drill now
could save lives later!**